TOM BRADY

BY MARTY GITLIN

Published by ABDO Publishing Company, PO Box 398166, Minneapolis, MN 55439. Copyright © 2012 by Abdo Consulting Group, Inc. International copyrights reserved in all countries. No part of this book may be reproduced in any form without written permission from the publisher. SportsZone™ is a trademark and logo of ABDO Publishing Company.

Printed in the United States of America,
North Mankato, Minnesota
092011
012012

 THIS BOOK CONTAINS AT LEAST 10% RECYCLED MATERIALS.

Editor: Chrös McDougall
Copy Editor: Anna Comstock
Series Design: Craig Hinton
Cover and Interior Production: Kazuko Collins

Photo Credits: Greg Trott/AP Images, cover, 1; Steven Senne/AP Images, 4; Doug Mills/ AP Images, 7; Tony Gutierrez/AP Images, 8; NFL/AP Images, 10; Carlos Osorio/AP Images, 13; Daniel Mears/AP Images, 15; Jim Rogash/AP Images, 16; David Drapkin/AP Images, 19, 25; Lisa Poole/AP Images, 21; Elise Amendola/AP Images, 22; Paul Spinelli/ AP Images, 27; Charles Krupa/AP Images, 29

Library of Congress Cataloging-in-Publication Data

Gitlin, Marty.
  Tom Brady : super bowl quarterback / by Marty Gitlin.
     p. cm. — (Playmakers)
  Includes bibliographical references and index.
  ISBN 978-1-61783-290-1
  1. Brady, Tom, 1977—Juvenile literature. 2. Quarterbacks (Football—United States—Biography—Juvenile literature. 3. Football players—United States—Biography—Juvenile literature. I. Title.
  GV939.B685G55 2012
  796.332092—dc23
  [B]
                              2011039537

TABLE OF CONTENTS

Tom Brady

CHAPTER 1

SUPER BEGINNINGS

Few people expected to see the New England Patriots in Super Bowl XXXVI. Even fewer people expected to see quarterback Tom Brady leading them. Starting quarterback Drew Bledsoe was injured in the season's second game. Tom took over. Not many people knew who he was. But he won 11 of 14 games as the starter.

Tom then led the Patriots to the Super Bowl. But the Patriots were in trouble. They once had a 14-point

Tom Brady led the Patriots to an 11–5 record in 2001. It was only his second season.

lead over the St. Louis Rams. But the score was tied 17–17 in the fourth quarter. Tom needed to do something. And he did. He drove the Patriots to the Rams' 30-yard line. Kicker Adam Vinatieri then kicked the game-winning field goal. Tom Brady's time of greatness in the National Football League (NFL) had begun.

> Tom has three older sisters. All of them were talented athletes growing up. Their names were in the newspaper so often that he was referred to as "The Little Brady." Tom got fed up with that nickname. So he wrote a paper for school stating that one day they would be known as Tom Brady's sisters.

Tom was not much of a football player growing up. He was born on August 3, 1977, in San Mateo, California. Many thought his future looked brightest in baseball. Tom was a talented catcher at Serra High School. He once smashed two home runs in a playoff game. And the Montreal Expos of Major League Baseball even drafted him in 1995. A draft is when teams in a league select incoming players.

Tom marches the Patriots down the field against the St. Louis Rams during Super Bowl XXXVI.

Tom loved football more than baseball. But he did not show as much promise on the football field. Tom began playing football as a ninth grader. He struggled to find playing time on an already bad team. Some people thought he was too slow. But that did not stop him. Tom worked hard. He finally became the starting quarterback as a junior. Tom was good. But few people thought he was great. He led his teams to 6–4 and 5–5

Tom Brady

Tom has always loved to jump rope. He jumped rope all the time growing up. It helped keep him fit for football. In fact, it still keeps Tom in shape. He can often be found jumping rope today.

records. University of Southern California coach John Robinson had once attended Serra. But he did not believe Tom was good enough to receive a full college scholarship.

Tom believed in himself, though. He was not one to brag during his youth. But he was quietly confident. He once told his mother that he would someday be a household name. His family simply laughed. They could never imagine what Tom would do years later in the Super Bowl. But Tom never gave up. He found a college team that believed in him, too. He decided to play for the University of Michigan. But Tom would once again have an uphill battle.

Tom celebrates after leading the Patriots to victory in Super Bowl XXXVI following the 2001 season.

Tom Brady

CHAPTER 2

PROVING HIMSELF WORTHY

Michigan is known for its strong football teams. Any starting player has to be really good. So, Tom Brady knew he had to earn his playing time.

Brady played in only two games as a freshman. He threw just five total passes. Michigan won the national championship the second year, in 1997. Brady played in four games that season. Still, he threw only 15 passes. And he had not yet thrown for a touchdown.

Brady was a two-time All-Big Ten Conference quarterback for the Michigan Wolverines.

Brady finally got his chance as a junior. Michigan's starting quarterback had graduated. But there was a battle to decide the new one. Michigan had another talented quarterback named Drew Henson. Many thought he could someday play pro football and pro baseball.

But Brady beat out Henson for the starting job. He led Michigan to wins in 10 of its last 11 games. Included was a 45–31 win over the University of Arkansas in the Citrus Bowl. The top teams in the nation get to end their season in bowl games.

Brady showed he could be a good college football player. But many scouts did not think he was good enough to play in the NFL. He had a strong enough arm. But scouts thought Brady was simply too slow. It took one great game to begin changing minds.

Some Michigan fans were worried after Brady's first two starts at quarterback. The team lost to both Notre Dame and Syracuse to start the season. The fans wanted coach Lloyd Carr to bench Brady. But Carr stuck with him. Brady won 10 of 11 games the rest of the 1998 season.

Brady beat out Drew Henson, *left*, and Jason Kapsner, *center*, to become the Wolverines' starting quarterback in 1998.

The Orange Bowl is one of the biggest bowl games. Michigan played the University of Alabama there in 2000. Both schools had great football teams. Brady had led his team to a 10–2 record that season. The Wolverines also beat their rival, Ohio State. But Michigan struggled against Alabama.

Brady did not let his team stay down for long, though. Michigan went down by 14 points twice. And Brady brought them back both times. That sent the game into overtime. Brady was the hero. He threw a 25-yard touchdown pass to tight end Shawn Thompson. That gave Michigan the win.

Brady completed 34 of 46 passes that day. He threw for four touchdowns. And he threw for a school bowl-game record of 369 yards. Brady was finally opening some eyes. Some people thought that game started his NFL career. They did not think he would be drafted before that game.

Brady's play might have gotten him into the NFL Draft. But it was not enough to make him a high draft pick. Brady thought a team might select him in the second or third round. He watched the draft on television with his father. They waited as teams picked player after player before Brady. The wait was hard. He had to go for a walk with his parents to get rid of the stress.

One quarterback was selected in the first round. And six quarterbacks were selected ahead of Brady. In fact, 198 players were selected before Brady. But finally, the New England Patriots picked him in the sixth round. The experience stayed with Brady for years to come.

Brady, *center*, celebrates with Michigan teammates and coach Lloyd Carr, *right*, after winning the 2000 Orange Bowl.

The Patriots took a chance on Brady. Sixth-round picks have a lot to prove. Many of them do not even make the team. Making the team as a quarterback is even harder. But Brady had proven people wrong before. And he was ready to do it again.

Tom Brady

CHAPTER 3

INTELLIGENCE, COMPASSION, AND HEART

Ian Gold thought Tom Brady was going to star in the NFL. He was Brady's teammate at Michigan. He knew that Brady was not fast or quick. But he also knew something else. Gold said Brady was always the smartest player on the field.

Brady did not play much as a rookie. But his intelligence showed during his second year. Drew Bledsoe was the Patriots' starting quarterback. But he was injured in the season's second game.

Brady directs his teammates before starting a play during the 2004 playoffs.

So Brady started the third game. He was still not the most athletic quarterback. But he never gave up that job. And he was able to lead his team to the Super Bowl title.

Even so, some people still questioned Brady. The Patriots finished 9–7 the next year. That was a winning record. But they missed the playoffs. Brady played injured for much of the year. The Patriots then began the 2003 season 2–2. Nobody was questioning Brady in the weeks that followed. He led New England to 12 straight wins to end the season. The Patriots then marched back to the Super Bowl.

New England played the Carolina Panthers in the Super Bowl. Brady threw for 354 yards and three touchdowns. The game again came down to the end. And Brady again starred under pressure. He led the Patriots down the field on a last-minute drive. Patriots kicker Adam Vinatieri again made a

Brady had a tough off-season following his first Super Bowl win. He had become a star. So, he was asked to make many public appearances. He also had to recover from shoulder surgery. Some believe the injury played a role in his disappointing 2002 season.

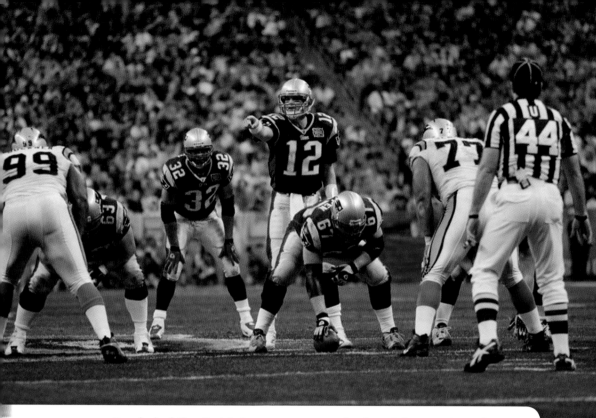

Brady led the Patriots on a game-winning drive against the Carolina Panthers in Super Bowl XXXVIII.

game-winning field goal. The Patriots won 32–29. Brady was not voted into the Pro Bowl that year. That is the NFL's All-Star game. But he was named the Super Bowl's Most Valuable Player.

Many said it was one of the most exciting endings in Super Bowl history. Brady called it a dream come true. Few people believed he would ever be an NFL quarterback. Now he was an NFL star. And he was just getting started.

Brady has been involved with a charity called Bikes for Best Buddies. He was named honorary chairman of the 2009 cycling event. Sports and entertainment celebrities participated. All money raised went to help people with mental disabilities.

A strong arm and great accuracy lead Brady on the football field. Kindness leads him off the field. Brady has worked with many charities over the years. Some of his work has been in Africa. He once traveled to Ghana and Uganda to help fight hunger and disease there. He has also aided the Active Force Foundation. It creates sports equipment for the disabled.

Brady has spent the most time focusing on children in need. He grew up in a wealthy neighborhood. But he saw how his fame and his story affected people. Brady hoped his story would inspire others to overcome steep odds as well. As Brady continued to star for the Patriots, his fame only grew.

Brady and teammate Tedy Bruschi pose with a fan at a Bikes for Best Buddies charity event at Harvard Stadium.

Tom Brady

CHAPTER 4

A FORCE ON THE FIELD

Most NFL teams have won at least one Super Bowl. A few have won two in a row. But keeping up success in the NFL is very hard. Few teams are able to win a lot of Super Bowls in a short time. Those who do are known as dynasties.

Many people thought the Patriots could be a dynasty going into the 2004 season. They had won two Super Bowls in three years. And they were favorites to win another one. But dynasties are not

Brady runs for a first down against the Chicago Bears during the 2006 season.

made on paper. The Patriots would have to go out and actually win. And that is exactly what they did.

The Patriots won their first six games. They finished the regular season with a 14–2 record. The team had many great players. But Brady was the biggest star. He made the offense unstoppable. They scored at least 20 points in every game but one.

Brady and the Patriots continued to play well in the playoffs. They easily beat the Indianapolis Colts and the Pittsburgh Steelers. A Super Bowl game against the Philadelphia Eagles was set.

Brady had always played well when it mattered most. And he did it again against the Eagles. He threw two touchdown passes and no interceptions. He led his team to two scoring drives in the fourth quarter. The Patriots beat the Eagles 24–21.

Brady led the Patriots to a Super Bowl victory in 2005 with a heavy heart. His grandmother had died that week and his father was in the hospital. Brady had played in the conference championship game two weeks earlier with a 103-degree fever.

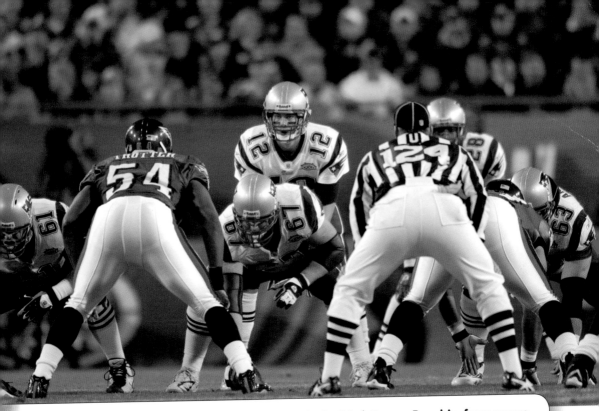

Brady and the Patriots won their third Super Bowl in four years when they beat the Philadelphia Eagles in Super Bowl XXXIX.

The Patriots had indeed won three Super Bowls in four years. Brady was asked after the victory if his team was a dynasty. He is not one to brag, though. So he said it was not the Patriots' style to declare their team a dynasty.

New England continued to be a top team. Brady led the Patriots to 10–6 and 12–4 records over the next two seasons. They reached the playoffs both times. Brady even led the NFL

Many people who knew nothing about football learned about Brady by 2009. That is when he married supermodel Gisele Bundchen in Los Angeles, California. The two married in a private ceremony in late February.

in passing yards in 2005. But New England fell short of a Super Bowl both seasons.

Most people agreed that Brady was a top NFL quarterback by then. The Patriots were also widely thought of as the best team of that time. But the 2007 Patriots team went down as one of the best teams ever. And Brady led the way.

No team scored as many points as the Patriots that season. They scored at least 34 points in each of their first eight games. They also averaged 50 points over one three-game period. New England had one of the best defenses in the league, too. That made the team a nearly unstoppable opponent. The Patriots finished the regular season with a 16–0 record. They became the first team in NFL history to do that.

Brady enjoyed one of the best seasons a quarterback has ever had. He had a league-high 4,806 passing yards. That was nearly 700 more yards than he had in 2005. He had also led the

Wide receiver Randy Moss, *left*, caught 23 of Brady's NFL-record 50 touchdown passes in 2007.

league in passing yards that year. But maybe the most amazing stat was Brady's 50 touchdown passes. That led the NFL. It also set a new NFL record. And, he only threw eight interceptions.

Nobody could stop New England during the regular season. It looked like nobody would be able to stop the team in the playoffs either. The Patriots cruised all the way to the Super Bowl. They just had to beat the New York Giants to complete the perfect season. Only the 1972 Miami Dolphins had completed a perfect season before. Many believed the Patriots would soon join them.

But it was not to be. The Giants held Brady to 266 passing yards and one touchdown. New England had scored at least 20 points in every game that season and postseason. But the Giants beat them 17–14 in the Super Bowl.

Still, Brady had played a good game. He threw a late touchdown pass to Randy Moss. It put the Patriots up with less than three minutes to play. But the Giants roared back to win it.

Brady refused to blame himself or his teammates for the defeat. He said the team had prepared well. They worked hard during the game, too.

Brady did not have a chance to make up for the loss in 2008. He was injured in the season's first game. The injury caused him to miss the entire season. It was the only time New

Brady has done many things well during his NFL career. Perhaps his best quality has been his accuracy. From 2001 to 2010, he has completed at least 60 percent of his passes every year.

Brady has proven throughout his career that he should never be written off.

England missed the playoffs from 2003 to 2010. Brady was back to lead his team in 2009 and 2010. He was still one of the NFL's top quarterbacks. He even led the league with 36 touchdowns in 2010. But the Patriots lost their first playoff game each season.

Brady was disappointed that he could not win another championship during those years. But if he has shown anything over the years, it is to never count him out.

FUN FACTS AND QUOTES

- Tom Brady and his family were huge fans of their hometown San Francisco 49ers when he was growing up. His sister Maureen later could not believe that her brother was being compared to 49ers Hall of Fame quarterback Joe Montana. "Our family worshiped Joe Montana," she said.

- When Brady was a child, he enjoyed getting autographs of famous athletes. Two very different experiences had a big effect on him. San Francisco 49ers superstar quarterback Joe Montana once took time to speak with Brady while signing an autograph. But Brady also asked San Francisco Giants star outfielder Chili Davis for an autograph and was turned down. Brady carried both moments with him into his adult life. He now makes a point to almost always sign autographs for kids when asked.

- About a month after leading the Patriots to the Super Bowl title, Brady headed to Gary, Indiana, for the Miss USA 2002 beauty pageant. Brady was selected to be one of the judges for the contest.

- Brady was one of many star athletes to graduate from Serra High School. Among the others were baseball slugger Barry Bonds and Pro Football Hall of Famer Lynn Swann.

WEB LINKS

To learn more about Tom Brady, visit ABDO Publishing Company online at **www.abdopublishing.com**. Web sites about Brady are featured on our Book Links page. These links are routinely monitored and updated to provide the most current information available.

GLOSSARY

charity
Money given or work done to help people in need.

draft
A yearly event in which NFL teams select the top college football players.

drive
When a team on offense moves down the field.

dynasty
A team that experiences a great deal of success over a period of time.

interception
A pass thrown by a quarterback that is caught by a member of the opposing defense.

overtime
An extra session of football played when a game is tied after four quarters.

quarterback
The player on a football team who runs the offense. He takes the snap to start each play and can either run with the ball, hand it off, or throw it.

rookie
A first-year player in the NFL.

scholarship
Monetary assistance awarded to students to help them pay for school. Top athletes earn scholarships to represent a college through its sports teams.

scouts
People hired by a team who watch athletes to determine if the athletes might be a good fit for that team. Scouts also watch opposing teams to help their team prepare for games.

INDEX

FURTHER RESOURCES

Doeden, Matt. *Tom Brady (Sports Heroes and Legends)*. Breckenridge, CO:
    Twenty-First Century Books, 2009.

Motzko, Mary. *New England Patriots*. Edina, MN: ABDO Publishing Co., 2011.

Price, Christopher. *New England Patriots: The Complete Illustrated History*.
    Minneapolis, MN: MVP Books, 2010.